To:

For:

From:

Date:

Christ's Christmas Season

By

Karen H Palmer

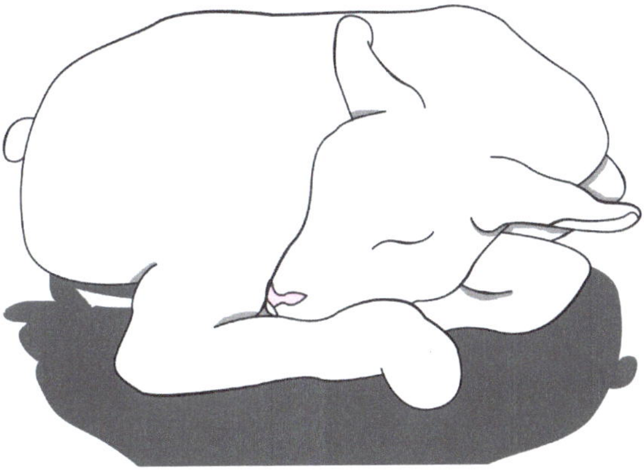

Illustrations

By

John Moore Chapman

Scripture taken from the Holy Bible King James Version

Published by
Christian Concepts for Kids, Inc.
228 Hawley Creek Road
Prosperity, SC 29127
www.christianconceptsforkids.com

Editing by Susan Klamroth Shami

Printed in the United States of America
(Ingram Sparks) Printing: 2025

This book is dedicated to
our Savior, Jesus Christ,
the true reason for
this Christmas season.

‘Twas the night before Christmas,
when all through the land
not a creature was stirring,
not even the lamb.

Everyone traveled
back to his hometown.
There were taxes to pay
and people to count.

Joseph and Mary,
no bed could they find.

They lay down to rest
where the animals dined.

Baby Jesus was born
there;
it could not be stopped.

In a manger He lay,
wrapped in swaddling
cloth.

Shepherds came by
just to visit the babe.
Angels rejoiced
at the plans God had
made.

The Wise Men read
of the blessed baby's
birth.

They followed a star
as they traveled the
Earth.

They brought Jesus gifts:
Gold! Frankincense! Myrrh!

For Jesus was born
as our blessing on Earth.

And that is
what happened
the first
Christmas
morn.

God's son, "God
Is With Us,"
Baby Jesus was
born!

So repent and believe
for your debt has been paid!

Paid in full!
Yes, in full,
all your sins
washed away!

With Him up in
Heaven
some day we will go.

Our worship and praises we'll sing 'round His home.

Jesus, the Lamb,
He came for a reason.
Yes, THIS is the story of
Christ's
Christmas Season.

This is the Christmas story as told by Matthew and Luke in the King James Version of the Bible..

Luke 1:26-38

26 And in the sixth month the angel Gabriel was sent from God unto a city of Galilee, named Nazareth, 27 To a virgin espoused to a man whose name was Joseph, of the house of David; and the virgin's name was Mary. 28 And the angel came in unto her, and said, Hail, thou that art highly favoured, the Lord is with thee: blessed art thou among women. 29 And when she saw him, she was troubled at his saying, and cast in her mind what manner of salutation this should be. 30 And the angel said unto her, Fear not, Mary: for thou hast found favour with God. 31 And, behold, thou shalt conceive in thy womb, and bring forth a son, and shalt call his name JESUS. 32 He shall be great, and shall be called the Son of the Highest: and the Lord God shall give unto him the throne of his father David: 33 And he shall reign over the house of Jacob for ever; and of his kingdom there shall be no end. 34 Then said Mary unto the angel, How shall this be, seeing I know not a man? 35 And the angel answered and said unto her, The Holy Ghost shall come upon thee, and the power of the Highest shall overshadow thee: therefore also that holy thing which shall be born of thee shall be called the Son of God. 36 And, behold, thy cousin Elisabeth, she hath also conceived a son in her old age: and this is the sixth month with her, who was called barren. 37 For with God nothing shall be impossible. 38 And Mary said, Behold the handmaid of the Lord; be it unto me according to thy word. And the angel departed from her.

Matthew 1:18-25

18 Now the birth of Jesus Christ was on this wise: When as his mother Mary was espoused to Joseph, before they came together, she was found with child of the Holy Ghost. 19 Then Joseph her husband, being a just man, and not willing to make her a publick example, was minded to put her away privily. 20 But while he thought on these things, behold, the angel of the Lord appeared unto him in a dream, saying, Joseph, thou son of David, fear not to take unto thee Mary thy wife: for that which is conceivedb in her is of the Holy Ghost. 21 And she shall bring forth a son, and thou shalt call his name JESUSc: for he shall save his people from their sins. 22 Now all this was done, that it might be fulfilled which was spoken of the Lord by the prophet, saying, 23 Behold, a virgin shall be with child,† and shall bring forth a son, and they shall call his name Emmanuel, which being interpreted is, God with us. 24 Then Joseph being raised from sleep did as the angel of the Lord had bidden him, and took unto him his wife: 25 And knew her not till she had brought forth her firstborn son: and he called his name JESUS.

Luke 2:1-20

1 And it came to pass in those days, that there went out a decree from Caesar
Augustus, that all the world should be taxeda. 2 (And this taxing was first made
when Cyrenius was governor of Syria.) 3 And all went to be taxedb, every one into
his own city. 4 And Joseph also went up from Galilee, out of the city of Nazareth,
into Judaea, unto the city of David, which is called Bethlehem; (because he was
of the house and lineage of David:) 5 To be taxedc with Mary his espoused wife,
being great with child. 6 And so it was, that, while they were there, the days were
accomplished that she should be delivered. 7 And she brought forth her firstborn
son, and wrapped him in swaddling clothes, and laid him in a manger; because
there was no room for them in the inn.
8 And there were in the same country shepherds abiding in the field, keeping
watchd over their flock by night. 9 And, lo, the angel of the Lord came upon them,
and the glory of the Lord shone round about them: and they were sore afraid.
10 And the angel said unto them, Fear not: for, behold, I bring you good tidings
of great joy, which shall be to all people. 11 For unto you is born this day in the
city of David a Saviour, which is Christ the Lord. 12 And this shall be a sign unto
you; Ye shall find the babe wrapped in swaddling clothes, lying in a manger. 13
And suddenly there was with the angel a multitude of the heavenly host praising
God, and saying, 14 Glory to God in the highest, and on earth peace, good will
toward men. 15 And it came to pass, as the angels were gone away from them into
heaven, the shepherdse said one to another, Let us now go even unto Bethlehem,
and see this thing which is come to pass, which the Lord hath made known unto
us. 16 And they came with haste, and found Mary, and Joseph, and the babe
lying in a manger. 17 And when they had seen it, they made known abroad the
saying which was told them concerning this child. 18 And all they that heard it
wondered at those things which were told them by the shepherds. 19 But Mary
kept all these things, and pondered them in her heart. 20 And the shepherds
returned, glorifying and praising God for all the things that they had heard and
seen, as it was told unto them.

Matthew 2:1-12

1 Now when Jesus was born in Bethlehem of Judaea
in the days of Herod the king, behold, there came wise
men from the east to Jerusalem, 2 Saying, Where is he
that is born King of the Jews? for we have seen his star
in the east, and are come to worship him. 3 When Herod the king had heard these
things, he was troubled, and all Jerusalem with him. 4 And when he had gathered
all the chief priests and scribes of the people together, he demanded of them

where Christ should be born. 5 And they said unto him, In Bethlehem of Judaea:
for thus it is written by the prophet, 6 And thou Bethlehem, in the land of Juda,
art not the least among the princes of Juda: for out of thee shall come a Governor,
that shall rulea my people Israel. 7 Then Herod, when he had privily called the
wise men, enquired of them diligently what time the star appeared. 8 And he sent
them to Bethlehem, and said, Go and search diligently for the young child; and
when ye have found him, bring me word again, that I may come and worship him
also.
9 When they had heard the king, they departed; and, lo, the star, which they saw
in the east, went before them, till it came and stood over where the young child
was. 10 When they saw the star, they rejoiced with exceeding great joy. 11 And
when they were come into the house, they saw the young child with Mary his
mother, and fell down, and worshipped him: and when they had opened their
treasures, they presentedb unto him gifts; gold, and frankincense, and myrrh. 12
And being warned of God in a dream that they should not return to Herod, they
departed into their own country another way.

Matthew 3:1-3

1 In those days came John the Baptist, preaching in the wilderness of Judaea,
2 And saying, Repent ye: for the kingdom of heaven is at hand. 3 For this is he
that was spoken of by the prophet Esaias, saying, The voice of one crying in the
wilderness, Prepare ye the way of the Lord, make his paths straight.

www.ingramcontent.com/pod-product-compliance
Lightning Source LLC
Chambersburg PA
CBHW041725070526
44586CB00001B/9
9781936733026